EXPLORING COUNTRIES

Egypt

by Walter Simmons

BELLWETHER MEDIA · MINNEAPOLIS, MN

Note to Librarians, Teachers, and Parents:

Blastoff! Readers are carefully developed by literacy experts and combine standards-based content with developmentally appropriate text.

Level 1 provides the most support through repetition of high-frequency words, light text, predictable sentence patterns, and strong visual support.

Level 2 offers early readers a bit more challenge through varied simple sentences, increased text load, and less repetition of high-frequency words.

Level 3 advances early-fluent readers toward fluency through increased text and concept load, less reliance on visuals, longer sentences, and more literary language.

Level 4 builds reading stamina by providing more text per page, increased use of punctuation, greater variation in sentence patterns, and increasingly challenging vocabulary.

Level 5 encourages children to move from "learning to read" to "reading to learn" by providing even more text, varied writing styles, and less familiar topics.

Whichever book is right for your reader, Blastoff! Readers are the perfect books to build confidence and encourage a love of reading that will last a lifetime!

This edition first published in 2011 by Bellwether Media, Inc.

No part of this publication may be reproduced in whole or in part without written permission of the publisher. For information regarding permission, write to Bellwether Media, Inc., Attention: Permissions Department, 6012 Blue Circle Drive, Minnetonka, MN 55343.

Library of Congress Cataloging-in-Publication Data

Simons, Walter (Walter G.)
Egypt / by Walter Simons.
   p. cm. – (Blastoff! readers) (Blastoff! readers)
Summary: "Developed by literacy experts for students in grades three through seven, this book introduces young readers to the geography and culture of Egypt. Provided by publisher.
Includes bibliographical references and index.
ISBN 978-1-60014-478-3 (hardcover : alk. paper)
1. Egypt–Juvenile literature. I. Title.
DT49.S55 2010
962–dc22   2010011412

080110   1162

Contents

Where Is Egypt?

Mediterranean Sea

Libya

Israel

Suez Canal

Cairo ★

Sinai Peninsula

Gulf of Suez

Gulf of Aqaba

Egypt

Red Sea

Nile River

Sudan

Egypt is a country in northeastern Africa that covers 386,662 square miles (1,001,450 square kilometers). The capital and largest city of Egypt is Cairo, which lies on the banks of the Nile River. Egypt borders Libya to the west, Sudan to the south, and Israel to the northeast.

Egypt's long northern coast faces the Mediterranean Sea. The Red Sea lies off Egypt's eastern coast. In the northeast, the Sinai **Peninsula** touches the **Gulf** of Suez to the west and the Gulf of Aqaba to the east.

Egypt is a flat country with deserts and rocky plains. The Sahara Desert covers most of Egypt. Egyptians know the desert region as the "red land." There are no towns in the desert except where **oases** exist around springs of water.

A narrow ribbon of green winds down the eastern side of Egypt. This is the Nile River Valley. People have lived in this valley for thousands of years. East of the Suez **Canal** is the Sinai Peninsula. Mountains rise in the southern part of the peninsula. North of the mountains lies the Sinai Desert, where there is not enough water for many people to live.

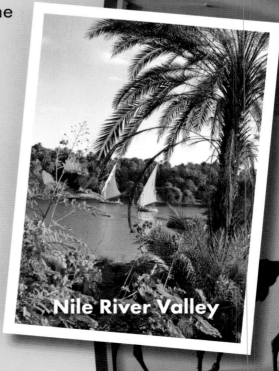

Nile River Valley

![!]

fun fact

Strong winds blow across the Sahara Desert. They can create hills of sand, called dunes, that are more than 100 feet (30.5 meters) high.

Sahara Desert

Did you know?

The Sinai Peninsula had some of the first mines ever built. They produced a deep blue-green stone known as turquoise. Long ago, the people living on the Sinai called it the "Land of Turquoise."

fun fact

Traditional Egyptian boats called *feluccas* have sailed the Nile for thousands of years.

Egypt depends on the Nile River for fresh water, **fertile** land, and transportation. There are only a few bridges that cross the river. In many places, small ferryboats carry people across. In the north, the Nile branches into smaller streams. These waterways form the Nile **Delta**, where the waters of the Nile empty into the Mediterranean Sea.

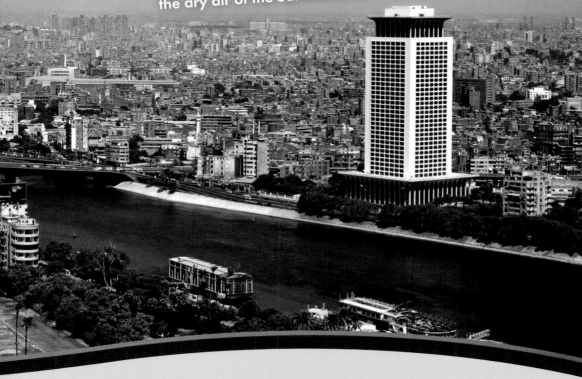

Did you know?

Most rivers grow wider as they flow toward the sea, but the Nile River gets narrower. No smaller streams join it, and much of its water evaporates into the dry air of the Sahara Desert.

In southern Egypt, the Aswan High Dam controls the flow of the Nile. Behind the dam is a **reservoir** known as Lake Nasser. The reservoir captures extra water when the Nile floods. When the water level of the Nile is low, the dam opens to allow more water to flow downstream.

crocodile

Egypt has abundant wildlife along the Nile and in the desert. Crocodiles lurk in the **wetlands** near the river. Nile perch swim in the river. These fish can grow up to 6 feet (2 meters) long and can weigh 500 pounds (227 kilograms). Several kinds of birds nest in the Nile Delta, including herons, egrets, and ibises. Many birds from Europe **migrate** to the delta during the winter.

Did you know?
Small, wild cats still prowl in the Nile Delta and along the Nile River Valley. The people of ancient Egypt were the first to tame these cats and make them their pets.

Nile perch

beetle

gazelle

In the Sahara, hyenas and desert foxes hunt for prey. Wild dogs howl while gazelles gallop over the dunes. Snakes, hedgehogs, rats, and other animals move across the hot desert sand. To hide from predators, beetles, scorpions, and other insects scurry under rocks.

Over 80 million people live in Egypt. Most of them have **ancestors** who lived in ancient Egypt over 2,000 years ago. Egyptians speak Arabic and use Arabic script to write their language. The people of Cairo speak their own **dialect**, called Cairene. This is the language used in newspapers and on television.

Speak Arabic!

Egyptians use Arabic script when they write. However, Arabic words can be written in English to help you read them out loud.

English	Arabic	How to say it
hello	ahlan	AH-lon
good-bye	ma'is salaama	mah-as sah-LE-mah
yes	aiwa	EYE-wah
no	la	lah
please (male)	low samaht	low sa-MAHT
please (female)	low samahti	low sa-MAHT-ee
thank you	shukran	SHU-krahn
friend (male)	saahib	SAAH-hib
friend (female)	sahba	SAH-bah

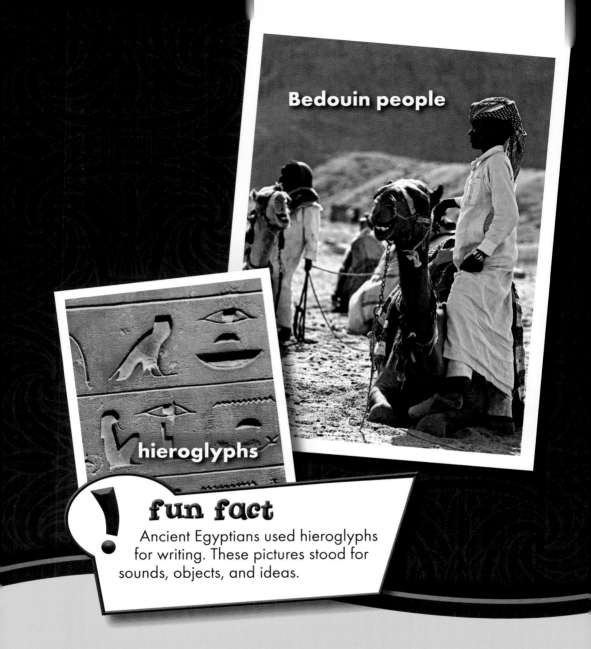

Bedouin people

hieroglyphs

fun fact

Ancient Egyptians used hieroglyphs for writing. These pictures stood for sounds, objects, and ideas.

The Bedouin people have lived in the desert for thousands of years. They are nomads who roam from place to place. Some have settled in small towns. Others still live in tents made of goatskin. They keep herds of camels and goats.

Did you know?

Cairo has huge street markets, or *souks*, where people can shop for goods. Some of these markets have been open for hundreds of years.

Egyptians leave their homes early in the morning. They walk, bike, or take buses or trains to get to school or work. Around midday, many workers return home for a meal. During the hot afternoon, the cities and towns are quiet. As the sun sinks and the temperature drops, Egyptians return to the streets. Small shops are open for business. Customers bargain with shop owners over clothing, shoes, and food.

Where People Live in Egypt

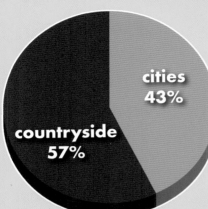

cities 43%

countryside 57%

In the countryside, families live in homes made of brick and plaster. Many of these homes have courtyards where people work and cook. During the summer, some people sleep on their rooftops to feel the cool, fresh air.

The law in Egypt requires children to attend school from ages 6 to 14. Elementary school lasts five years, and then students move on to middle school. Students learn science, math, and other subjects in the Arabic language. Some schools teach classes in English. Classrooms are often crowded, and some have no textbooks or school supplies.

Some students drop out of school to work. Families in the countryside need their children to help with farm work. Students who do complete secondary school can apply to go to a university. They must pass a tough exam before they can attend.

Did you know?

Egyptian schools require students to dress in uniforms. Students often wear collared shirts with ties. Girls wear skirts and boys wear pants. For everyone in Egypt, shoulders must be covered.

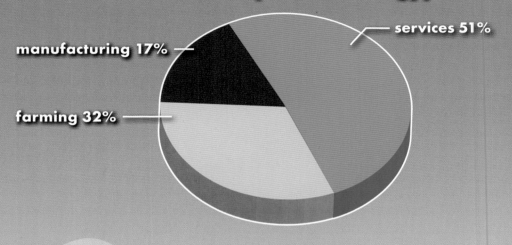

Where People Work in Egypt

services 51%

manufacturing 17%

farming 32%

Did you know?

Egypt ships its goods to many countries. Most go to Italy or the United States.

In Egyptian cities, factory workers make **textiles**, cement, fertilizers, and other goods. Some Egyptian companies produce electronic equipment. Many Egyptians have **service jobs** in hotels, restaurants, and shops.

Farming and mining are big industries in Egypt's countryside. Miners dig up iron ore, coal, and uranium. They also draw oil and natural gas out of the earth. Egyptian farmers rely on the waters of the Nile. They use water from canals to **irrigate** their fields of rice, barley, cotton, and other crops. Egypt sells its high-quality cotton all over the world.

backgammon

Did you know?
The ancient Egyptians played *Senet*, the oldest board game in the world. Backgammon is likely a modern version of *Senet*.

Egyptians like to spend their free time talking with and visiting their friends. They often meet in an *ahwa*, or coffee shop. In Cairo, people like to walk along the Nile or visit the zoo. They also enjoy trips to the seaside, where they can stay at resorts on the Mediterranean or the Red Sea.

Egyptians also like to play sports. Their favorite sport is soccer. Kids all over the country play soccer in streets, parks, and other open areas. Tennis, squash, and basketball are also popular sports.

fun fact

The Egyptian national soccer team, the Pharaohs, won the African Nations Cup in 2010.

Food

souk

Egyptian food is similar to food in other Middle Eastern countries. Most Egyptian meals include vegetables, which can be bought at colorful local *souks*. Many Egyptians have a plate of *ful medames* every day. For this dish, cooks boil fava beans with onions, parsley, and lemon juice. They fry the mix in olive oil and serve it with bread.

hummus and pita bread

kebabs

Another Egyptian favorite is the kebab. Pieces of spiced meat are speared on skewers, and then grilled over a flame. Egyptians eat vegetables, rice, and bread with their kebabs. Hummus combines mashed sesame seeds, mashed chickpeas, lemon juice, garlic, and olive oil. It makes a delicious spread for thin pita bread.

Revolution Day

On national holidays in Egypt, shops close and people stay home. Sinai Liberation Day takes place on April 25. This holiday celebrates a treaty with Israel that gave Egypt control of the Sinai Peninsula. On Revolution Day, Egyptians celebrate the founding of their modern **republic**. This holiday takes place on July 23.

Most Egyptians follow the religion of Islam. The dates of many religious holidays in Egypt follow the Islamic calendar. **Mawlid** celebrates the birth of the prophet Muhammad. This holiday occurs in the third month of the Islamic year. **Ramadan** is a holy month for Islam. This is a time of fasting, when Muslims eat only after sundown. At the end of Ramadan, families and friends gather for a big feast.

fun fact

Fawanees, or Ramadan lanterns, are important symbols of Ramadan in Egypt. Children often swing them in the streets while singing traditional Ramadan songs.

fawanees

Ancient Egyptians built many structures, including temples, monuments, and tombs. Several were built on the banks of the Nile near the modern city of Luxor. Many of these buildings are still standing today.

The ancient Egyptians buried many of their **pharaohs** in the desert hills across the river from Luxor. Some were also buried in the Pyramids of Giza, which were built more than 4,500 years ago. They still tower over a desert plain near the Sphinx, a sculpture with the body of a lion and the head of a pharaoh. These monuments were built to display the power of the pharaohs and the might of the Egyptian gods. Today, they keep Egyptians connected to their country's rich history and culture.

Sphinx

The Great Pyramid of Cheops is the largest pyramid in Egypt. Cheops originally contained 210 layers of stone blocks and about 2,500,000 blocks in all. Of the Seven Wonders of the Ancient World, it is the only one that is still standing.

Pyramids of Giza

← Cheops

Fast Facts About Egypt

Egypt's Flag

Egypt officially adopted its current flag in 1984. The flag has one red, one white, and one black stripe. In the center of the flag is the crest of Saladin, an ancient ruler of a kingdom that included Egypt. In the crest, a gold eagle perches on top of a banner that reads "Arab Republic of Egypt" in Arabic script.

Official Name: Arab Republic of Egypt

Area: 386,662 square miles (1,001,450 square kilometers); Egypt is the 30th largest country in the world.

Capital City:	Cairo
Important Cities:	Alexandria, Giza, Suez, Luxor
Population:	80,471,869 (July 2010)
Official Language:	Arabic
National Holiday:	Revolution Day (July 23)
Religions:	Muslim (90%), Christian (10%)
Major Industries:	farming, manufacturing, mining, services, tourism
Natural Resources:	oil, natural gas, iron ore, coal, uranium
Manufactured Products:	iron, steel, electronics, chemicals, construction materials, clothing, machinery
Farm Products:	cotton, wheat, dates, rice, citrus fruits, grapes, sugarcane, corn, barley
Unit of Money:	Egyptian pound; the pound is divided into 100 piastres.

Glossary

ancestors—relatives who lived long ago

canal—a trench dug across land that connects two bodies of water; canals allow ships to move between the two bodies of water.

delta—the area around the mouth of a river

dialect—a unique way of speaking a language; dialects are often specific to certain regions of a country.

fertile—supports growth

gulf—part of an ocean or sea that extends into land

irrigate—to bring water to a field of crops

Mawlid—the celebration of the birthday of the prophet Muhammad

migrate—to move from one place to another, often with the seasons

oases—fertile areas in an otherwise dry region, such as a desert; most oases surround a spring of water.

peninsula—a section of land that extends out from a larger piece of land and is almost completely surrounded by water

pharaohs—rulers of ancient Egypt

Ramadan—a religious holiday for Muslims that lasts a month

republic—a nation governed by elected leaders instead of a monarch

reservoir—a large lake formed behind a river dam

service jobs—jobs that perform tasks for people or businesses

textiles—materials that are made into clothing and other soft goods

wetlands—wet, spongy land; bogs, marshes, and swamps are wetlands.

To Learn More

AT THE LIBRARY

Bowden, Rob, and Roy Maconachie. *Cairo*. Milwaukee, Wisc.: World Almanac Library, 2005.

Heinrichs, Ann. *Egypt*. New York, N.Y.: Children's Press, 2007.

Steele, Philip. *Ancient Egypt*. New York, N.Y.: Rosen Publishing, 2009.

ON THE WEB

Learning more about Egypt is as easy as 1, 2, 3.

1. Go to www.factsurfer.com.

2. Enter "Egypt" into the search box.

3. Click the "Surf" button and you will see a list of related Web sites.

With factsurfer.com, finding more information is just a click away.

Index

The images in this book are reproduced through the courtesy of: Juan Martinez, front cover, pp. 8-9, 11 (middle & bottom), 13 (left), 26-27, 26 (small), 29 (bill & coin); Maisei Raman, front cover (flag), p. 28; Jon Eppard, pp. 4-5; Vladimir Wrangel, pp. 6-7; AMPhoto/Alamy, p. 6 (small); Christian Lindner, p. 8 (small); Christian Heinrich/Photolibrary, pp. 10-11; Angling Direct Holidays, p. 11 (top); Body Philippe/Photolibrary, p. 13 (right); Steve Starr/Photolibrary, p. 14; Josef Niedermeier/Photolibrary, p. 15; Boderlands/Alamy, pp. 16-17; Jacques Marais/Getty Images, p. 18; Frank Chmura/Photolibrary, p. 19 (left); Ana Menendez, p. 19 (right); Gavan Goulder/Photolibrary, p. 20; Jonathan Larsen, p. 21; Sylvain Grandadam/Getty Images, p. 22; Lisa Eastman, p. 23 (top); Martin Darley, p. 23 (bottom); Kordcom Kordcom/Photolibrary, p. 24; AFP/Getty Images, p. 25.